Bill Alexander has a flair for the spectacular in his painting. After many years in Canada, U.S.A. and Europe his style is unique and all his own. To receive the most from his step paintings you will have to follow each step closely and practice many times. If you say "Oh, that is easy," BOY have you a surprise, and you will find yourself in deep water, and saying, "I CAN'T." This is part of a poem I wrote for myself and to friends Christmas 1970, and I still use it. Ask anyone here at the office.

CAN'T

Can't is the father of feeble endeavor,
The parent of terror and half-hearted work;

It weakens the efforts of artisan clever,
And makes of the toiler an indolent shirk.

Can't is the word that is foe to ambition,
An enemy ambushed to shatter your will;

Hate it, with hatred that's deep and undying.
For once it is welcomed 'twill break any man;

What ever the goal you are seeking keep trying,
And answer this **demon** *by saying* **Damn** *it, I can!!"*

Have a nice day of painting. Bye.

Walter Foster

Clouds are painted with a dancing, swirling stroke. Paint is applied **only to one corner of the brush**; this yields a line of cloud against blue, blend away unwanted distinct outlines. When blending, use a very light stroke so that only the top hairs of the brush touch the painting. Remember: Always use as little paint as possible.

1

THIS TECHNIQUE IS **WET ON WET** (Light on dark.) Your canvas **must** be coated with a thin coat of oil white. You paint on the **wet White.**

ℱir and pine trees can be painted with either the 1″ brush or the palette knife. To use the brush, load it **heavily** so that it forms an edge, start at the top with a blotting stroke and work downward, fanning outwardly toward the base. With the knife, I also load it heavily and use more of a sidewise dabbing stroke, working again from the top down.

$\mathcal{S}$ummer sun comes soaring through mountain notches and winds down across wide valleys. My colors are Lemon Yellow, Cadmium Red, Alizarin Crimson, Prussian Blue, Flake White, Van Dyke Brown and Sap Green.

$\mathcal{S}$ ince the sky reflects into the water, the sky and water are put on at the same time in order to harmonize with each other. Blue sky is always brushed on **from the top downwards** with a large blending brush; likewise, water **from the bottom up.** This forms a horizon area and gives perspective. Always blend from the horizon area into the darker blue . . . never come back with a dirty brush.

W. ALEXANDER

Low-hanging clouds envelop distant snow-capped peaks which rise from a pine shrouded lagoon. Here is a good example of reflections in water, notice that trees and sky are reflected. Use Sap Green, Lemon Yellow, Flake White, Prussian Blue, Van Dyke Brown and Alizarin Crimson.

During that season called "**Autumn,**" the leaves of the vine maple color great stretches of Douglas fir, hemlock and cedar. Soon the leaves will fall and the birds will leave for warmer climates. My colors are: Sap Green, Prussian Blue, Lemon Yellow, Cadmium Red and Alizarin Crimson.

Shaggy scrub-brush and sparse trees struggle for survival against a background of wind-edged plateaus and fleecy clouds to produce this colorful desert array. I painted this scene with Alizarin Crimson, Prussian Blue, Flake White, Lemon Yellow, Van Dyke Brown, Cadmium Red and Viridian Green.

The canvas for land and seascape paintings is first prepared with a slow-drying, under-coat, white paint. Cover the canvas thoroughly with as thin a film of paint as possible, brushing with a large blending brush, horizontally and vertically several times. Note: Clean brush **thoroughly** in paint thinner and always shake and slap dry. It is very important to keep the brush as dry as possible.

he season is "**Spring**" and moisture-laden fog moves along a placid river and points to heights of majestic beauty. The sun is higher . . . and the magic of the season has touched every living thing. Use the colors Sap Green, Prussian Blue, Alizarin Crimson, Van Dyke Brown, Lemon Yellow, Cadmium Red and Flake White.

ecide where you want to have the sunlight hit the snow on the mountains and apply White to those areas with your knife. Start at the top of mountain and let knife float downward. Flake White paint will naturally break by itself, thus forming texture and character on your mountains. I usually blend a little Prussian Blue and Flake White for shade areas of snow. Finally, with a large blending brush, lightly blend from top downward.

S pectacular glacier-etched peaks overhang
magnificently above a deep clear pool to
yield an aura of dangerous beauty. The trees on
either side give balance to the painting and the cliff
road leads into the distance. To capture this dream
I used Flake White, Alizarin Crimson, Prussian Blue,
Sap Green, Van Dyke Brown, Cadmium Red and
Lemon Yellow.

always use colors for the middle ground that will provide a contrast between the background and foreground. Also, my colors are usually lighter and less vivid than my colors in the foreground. Distant trees can be formed with either the knife or 1″ brush. The trunks of the trees are made with a scratching stroke with the knife.

A stately old birch "monarch" conquers the scenic beauty of a mosaicly-carpeted winter floor composed of snow covered foliage, ice and reflecting water. The mountains stand guard over this peaceful scene and wait for spring to arrive. Use colors of Prussian Blue, Van Dyke Brown, Flake White, Sap Green, Alizarin Crimson and Viridian Green. Practice until you achieve a **cold** effect.

13

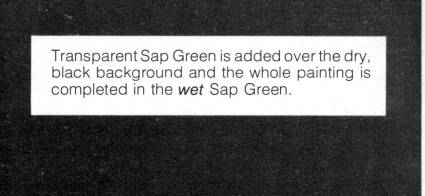

Canvas is painted *black* with *acrylic paint* and permitted to dry *completely*.

Transparent Sap Green is added over the dry, black background and the whole painting is completed in the *wet* Sap Green.

On the cool green depths of a virgin forest, early morning sunlight penetrates to colorfully illuminate selected foliage. With the background of Sap Green, highlight with colors of Lemon Yellow, Cadmium Red and Van Dyke Brown. This painting demonstrates the effectiveness of this light on dark technique.

Summer's early morning warmth along a distant mountain provides an interesting contrast to the coldness of a frozen hillside and brilliance of shore line vegetation. To paint this landscape I used Cadmium Red, Sap Green, Prussian Blue, Flake White, Lemon Yellow, Van Dyke Brown and Alizarin Crimson.

$\mathcal{I}$ normally use Prussian Blue, Alizarin Crimson, Van Dyke Brown and Flake White to color my mountains. Never over-mix the colors on the palette; they should yield a marble effect. With a knife and **very little paint** form the outline of the mountain against the sky, then scrape **downward.** Blend with a large brush from the sky downward and use the large brush to fade base of mountain into horizon.

$\mathcal{A}$ utumn colors mingle with evergreens and giant rock formations to help conceal a high range trail shelter. The colors I used to capture this mental dream are Prussian Blue, Sap Green, Lemon Yellow, Cadmium Red, Van Dyke Brown, Alizarin Crimson and Flake White.

Autumn foliage and evergreen forest reflect a colorful array onto a beautiful moss-layered lagoon. With your brush and canvas, such reveries become lasting enjoyment. Paint with Cadmium Red, Sap Green, Lemon Yellow, Prussian Blue, Flake White, Van Dyke Brown and Alizarin Crimson.

ext to the healing spirit of the high mountain country, my soul is refilled by the endless breaking of waves against rock and sand. There is majesty and beauty in both. Train your eye to see as an **artist;** things that were commonplace assume a new meaning and beauty. Paint this with Prussian Blue, Van Dyke Brown, Alizarin Crimson, Viridian and Flake White.

The leaves are gone and only the evergreens remain un-changed. Winter's bold face cloaks majestic peaks rising from a forest framed lake. Although the colors are the same,

Prussian Blue, Van Dyke Brown, Flake White, Alizarin Crimson and Sap Green, they can be blended to portray the winter scene and achieve a **cool** effect. Practice mixing your colors.

"SNOW CAPPED MOUNTAINS"

Snowcapped mountains see themselves in the lake below,
And their forceful image mingles softly with the water's flow.

Life-giving pure water flowed from these natural springs and helped sustain early western travelers. In this composition the spring is the central point of interest. The trees act as a dividing line between the mountains and the foreground, and are balanced by the evergreens on either side. I used: Lemon Yellow, Sap Green, Flake White, Van Dyke Brown, Alizarin and Cadmium Red.

Winter's generous mantle gracefully adorns clusters of pine trees along the frozen banks of a high alpine lake. Although my palette may seem restricted it proves one doesn't need a great number of colors to achieve many effects. Buy the best materials and **practice** with them. For instance, only Prussian Blue, Flake White, Alizarin Crimson and Sap Green were used to capture this scene.

Birch-type trees are painted with the knife and little paint using a side-action stroke **from the bottom skyward.** Foreground brush and low-lying foliage can be painted with either the knife or a 1″ brush; the brush with bristles spread full of paint is used in a **dabbing** stroke; foliage with the knife is made with a **light-floating downward** stroke. For ground area, I usually work with my palette knife loaded with different colors and a **sideways stroke.**

"ARTIST PARADISE"

The shady nook beside the brook, where water lilies rise,
Where birches sway and brook trout play, is Artist Paradise.

ow-hanging clouds shutter the effect of the evening sun as it reflects its blazing color into a vast sea and pine-shrouded cove. We are fast running out of wilderness and solitude, so capture colorful scenes like these on canvas while they are still here to enjoy. Paint this with Crimson, Prussian Blue, Van Dyke Brown, Lemon Yellow, Cadmium Red, Sap Green and Flake White.

W. ALEXANDER

Giant Ponderosa pine stand erect along a winding dirt road in late May. These sentinels have endured and embraced many seasons. They stand, a living testament, among the colors of the earth in spring. Paint this with Sap Green, Van Dyke Brown, Flake White, Cadmium Red, Prussian Blue and Lemon Yellow. Don't forget the shadows cast by the tree trunks across the road; these are important to your composition.

The poems that appear throughout my book (as well as the other lyrical descriptions) were written by my wife Annegret de Vries, writer and composer in her own right, and always an understanding and loyal critic. May this book encourage you to put your own dream on canvas.

Happy painting . . .

Bill Alexander

"AUTUMN WINDS"

Transformed from green to red and yellow, are Maple, Oak and Aspen trees.
The autumn wind sings soft and mellow,
His never ending melodies.

"CANDLE LIGHT & MEMORIES"

Candle light and memories,
A sentimental rhyme,
Are old fashioned symphonies,
And sweeter than old wine.

"REFLECTIONS"

The gentle autumn breeze, caresses blazing trees.
Along the shady river bank, reflections wander hand in hand.
And rising into gray-blue skies, the Meadowlark sings her good-byes.

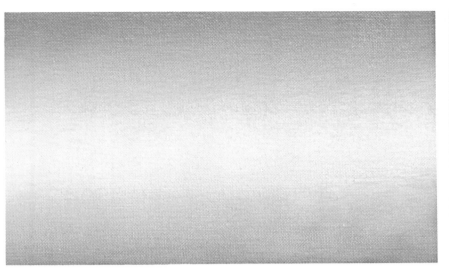

"PATCHES OF SNOW"

Billowing clouds over shimmering pools
Autumn is still aglow
But winter has already made his first step
Leaving patches of snow.

30

"A BY-GONE-DAY"

Shadows of a by-gone-day, linger everywhere,
Softly the winds are whispering, "Night is drawing near."

"THE SUN"

Before the sun can go to rest, she always tries to do her best.
She battles darkness brave and bold, and does not sleep until her world
Finds peace, beneath a cloak of gold.

This **"Mystic Mood"** was achieved by capturing the early morning solar rays that pierced the storm clouds to partially illumine the fields and stream.

I painted this with Van Dyke Brown, Prussian Blue, Lemon Yellow, Sap Green, Flake White, Alizarin Crimson and Cadmium Red.